MW01144298

Ray Edward **"Eddie" Coch**ı 1938, Albert Lea, Minnesota, U.S., was a Singer-songwriter and musician. Cochran's rockabilly songs, including "Twenty Flight Rock", "Summertime Blues", "C'mon Everybody" and "Somethin' Else", captured teenage frustration and desire during the mid-1950s to early 1960s.

Eddie experimented with multitrack recording, distortion techniques, and overdubbing from his earliest singles, having played the guitar, piano, bass, and drums. His image as a sharply dressed, good-looking young man with a rebellious attitude, epitomized the 1950s rocker, becoming of iconic status following his tragic early death.

Cochran was involved with music from when very young, playing in his school band, having taught himself to play blues guitar. Eddie formed a duet with the guitarist and songwriter, Hank Cochran, the pair recording as the Cochran Brothers, although they weren't related. Eddie then began a songwriting career with Jerry Capehart, his future manager, after splitting from Hank the following year. His breakthrough came when he performed the song "Twenty Flight Rock" in the musical comedy movie, The Girl Can't Help It, starring Jayne Mansfield, having signed a recording contract with Liberty Records soon afterwards.

Cochran died aged just 21, the day after a road accident on Rowden Hill, on Saturday, April 16th, while travelling in a taxi in Chippenham, Wiltshire, during his British tour of 1960, having just performed at Bristol's

Hippodrome theatre. Eddie's best-known songs were released during his lifetime, with more being issued posthumously, before he was inducted into the Rock and Roll Hall of Fame during 1987. Cochran's songs have been recorded by a wide variety of artists.

Ray Edward was the son of Alice and Frank R. Cochran, who were from Oklahoma. He took music lessons in school but left the band to play drums, also having begun learning the guitar, playing country and other music he heard on the radio. Eddie's family moved to Bell Gardens, California, during 1952. As his guitar playing improved, he formed a group with two friends from his junior high school, dropping out of Bell Gardens High School during his first year to become a professional musician.

During a show featuring many musicians at an American Legion hall, Eddie met Hank Cochran, a songwriter, the duo having begun performing together. Although they weren't related, they recorded as the Cochran Brothers, cutting a few singles for Ekko Records that were quite successful, having helped to establish them as a performing act.

Eddie also worked as a session musician, having begun writing songs, making a demo with Jerry Capehart, his future manager. Cochran's first "solo artist" single was released by Crest Records during July 1956, featuring "Skinny Jim", which came to be considered as a rock-and-roll and rockabilly classic. Boris Petroff asked Eddie during the spring of 1956, if he'd appear in the musical comedy film The Girl Can't Help It, Cochan performing the song "Twenty Flight Rock" in the movie.

Eddie starred in his second film, Untamed Youth during 1957, then had another hit, "Sittin' in the Balcony", by John D. Loudermilk, one of the few songs he recorded that was written by another songwriter. "Twenty Flight Rock" was written by AMI staff writer Nelda Fairchild, under the pen name Ned Fairchild. Nelda, who wasn't a rock and roll performer, provided the initial form of the song, the co-writing credit being a reflection of Cochran's major changes.

Eddie's only studio album issued during his lifetime, Singin' to My Baby, was released by Liberty Records during February 1957, having included "Sittin' in the Balcony". There were only a few rockers on the L.P., Liberty seemingly having wanted to move Cochran in a different musical direction, which he refused to do.

Later that year Eddie co-wrote the classic teenage anthem "Summertime Blues" with Jerry Capehart, which established him as one of the most important influences on rock 'n' roll of the 1950s, both lyrically and musically, the song, issued by Liberty recording no. 55144, charting at US # 8 during 1957. Cochran had a few more hits during his brief career, including "C'mon, Everybody", "Somethin' Else", "Teenage Heaven", then his posthumous UK chart-topper, "Three Steps to Heaven". Eddie remained popular in the US and UK through the late 1950s - early 1960s, with more posthumous hits, including "My Way", "Weekend", and "Nervous Breakdown".

Another facet of Cochran's short but brilliant career was his work as a backup musician and producer, having played lead guitar for Skeets McDonald at Columbia's studios on "You Oughta See Grandma Rock" and "Heart Breaking Mama". In a session for Gene Vincent during March 1958, Eddie contributed his trademark bass voice, as heard on "Summertime Blues", the records being issued on the album, A Gene Vincent Record Date.

Two of Cochran's friends, Buddy Holly and Ritchie Valens, along with the Big Bopper, were killed in a plane crash while on tour during early 1959. Eddie's friends and family later said that he was badly shaken by their deaths, having developed a morbid premonition that he'd also die young. Soon after their passing he recorded "Three Stars" in tribute to them, written by DJ Tommy Dee.

Cochran was keen to give up life on the road to spend his time in the studio making music, to avoid the chance of suffering a similar fatal accident while touring. However, Eddie's financial responsibilities meant that he continued to perform live, leading to his acceptance of an offer to tour the UK during 1960.

On Saturday, April 16th, 1960, c. 11.50 p.m., while on tour in the United Kingdom, the 21-year-old Cochran was involved in a road traffic accident, in a taxi travelling on the A4 through Chippenham, Wiltshire. The speeding taxi blew a tyre, so the driver lost control, with the car crashing into a lamppost on Rowden Hill, no other vehicle being involved.

Cochran, who was seated in the centre of the back seat, threw himself over his fiancée, songwriter Sharon Sheeley, to shield her, being thrown out of the car when the door flew open. Eddie was taken to St Martin's Hospital, in Bath, Somerset, where he died of severe head injuries at 4:10 p.m. the following day. Cochran's body was flown home, then his remains were buried on April 25th, 1960, at Forest Lawn Memorial Park, in Cypress, California.

Sharon Sheeley, tour manager Pat Thompkins, and singer Gene Vincent survived the crash, Vincent sustaining lasting injuries to his already permanently damaged leg, affecting him for the rest of his life, having cut short his career. The taxi driver, George Martin, unrelated to The Beatles producer George Martin, was convicted of dangerous driving, being fined £50 then when in default of payment, 6 months imprisonment, having also been disqualified from driving for 15 years. However, Martin apparently served no prison sentence, with his driving licence being reinstated 6 years early, during 1969.

The taxi was impounded at the local police station with other items from the crash, until a coroner's inquest could be held. David Harman, a police cadet at the station, later became known as Dave Dee of the band Dave Dee, Dozy, Beaky, Mick & Tich, having taught himself to play guitar on Eddie's impounded Gretsch.

A plaque was erected to mark the site of the crash on Rowden Hill, Chippenham, with a memorial stone commemorating Cochran also being placed in the old chapel grounds of St Martin's Hospital, in Bath, having been restored during 2010, on the 50th anniversary of his death. A memorial plaque was also placed next to the sundial at the back of the old chapel.

Cochran was a prolific performer, with a posthumous L.P., My Way, having released during 1964, the British label Rockstar Records going on to issue more of his music posthumously than was released during Eddie's lifetime, the company continuing to search for unpublished songs. One of his posthumous issues was "Three Stars", a tribute to J. P. Richardson, better known as the Big Bopper, and Cochran's friends Buddy Holly and Ritchie Valens, who'd all died in a plane crash just over a year before Eddie's end. Written just hours after the earlier tragedy by DJ Tommy Dee, it was recorded by Cochran two days later, Dee recording his own version several weeks later. Eddie's voice broke during the spoken lyrics about Valens and Holly.

Cochran was inducted into the Rock and Roll Hall of Fame during 1987, with his pioneering contribution to the genre of rockabilly having also been recognized by the Rockabilly Hall of Fame. Several of his songs have been re-released since his death, including "C'mon Everybody", which was a # 14 hit during 1988 in the UK.

Rolling Stone magazine ranked Eddie # 84 on its 2003 list of the 100 greatest guitarists of all time. Cochran's life has been chronicled in several publications, including Don't Forget Me: The Eddie Cochran Story, by

Julie Mundy and Darrel Higham (ISBN 0-8230-7931-7), and Three Steps to Heaven, by Bobby Cochran (ISBN 0-634-03252-6). The Very Best of Eddie Cochran was released by EMI Records on June 2nd, 2008. On September 27th, 2010, the mayor of Bell Gardens, California, declared his birthday of October 3rd, to be "Eddie Cochran Day," to celebrate the famous musician who began his career when living in that city.

Cochran was one of the first rock 'n' roll artists to write his own songs and overdub tracks, having also been one of the first to use an unwound third string to "bend" notes up a whole tone. It was an innovation that became an essential part of the standard rock guitar vocabulary, having been passed on to UK guitarist Joe Brown, who was thus given a lot of session work.

Artists including Joan Jett and the Blackhearts, the Rolling Stones, Bruce Springsteen, Van Halen, Tom Petty, Rod Stewart, T. Rex, Cliff Richard, the Who, the Beach Boys, the Beatles, Led Zeppelin, the White Stripes, the Sex Pistols, Sid Vicious, Rush, Simple Minds, George Thorogood, Guitar Wolf, Paul McCartney, Alan Jackson, the Move, David Bowie, Jimi Hendrix, Johnny Hallyday and U2 have covered Eddie's songs.

Paul McCartney knowing the chords and words to "Twenty Flight Rock" led to him becoming a member of the Beatles, John Lennon having been so impressed that he invited McCartney to play with his group, the Quarrymen. Jimi Hendrix performed "Summertime Blues" early in his career, with Pete Townshend of the

Who being heavily influenced by Cochran's guitar style, "Summertime Blues" having been a staple of live performances by the Who until the death of the bassist and vocalist John Entwistle during 2002, being featured on their album Live at Leeds.

The glam-rock artist Marc Bolan had his main Gibson Les Paul guitar refinished in a transparent orange, to resemble the Gretsch 6120 played by Eddie, who was his hero. He was also an influence on the guitarist Brian Setzer, of Stray Cats, who played a 6120 very similar to that of Cochran, whom he portrayed in the movie La Bamba.

Filmography

Year	Film	Role	Distributor
1956	The Girl Can't Help It	himself	20th Century Fox
1957	Untamed Youth	Bong	Warner Bros.
1959	Go, Johnny, Go	himself	Hal Roach Studios

Discography

Albums

US albums

Singin' to My Baby, Liberty LRP-3061 (mid-1957)

Eddie Cochran, Liberty LRP-3172 (April 1959), reissued as 12 of His Biggest Hits and later The Eddie Cochran Memorial Album

Never to Be Forgotten, Liberty LRP-3220 (January 1962)

Summertime Blues, Sunset SUS-5123 (August 1966)

Legendary Masters Series, United Artists UAS 9959 (January 1972)

The Very Best of Eddie Cochran (1975)

Great Hits (1983)

On the Air (1987)

The Best of Eddie Cochran (1987)

Greatest Hits, Curb Records (1990)

Singin' to My Baby and Never to Be Forgotten, EMI Records (1993)

UK albums

Singin' to My Baby (1957)

The Eddie Cochran Memorial Album (September 1960)

Cherished Memories (December 1962)

My Way (September 1964)

The Legendary Eddie Cochran (June 1971)

The Many Sides of Eddie Cochran (1974)

The Eddie Cochran Singles Album (August 1979)

20th Anniversary Album (March 1980)

The Best of Eddie Cochran, Liberty-EMI U.K. (1985) (the mono 16-track LP/cassette is from the Rock 'N' Roll Masters series)

The Very Best of Eddie Cochran (June 2008)

Eddie Cochran Story (July 6, 2009)

Singles

Year   Titles (A-side, B-side) Both sides from same album except where indicated.   Peak chart positions   US   UK   US Album

1954   "Two Blue Singin' Stars"   b/w "Mr. Fiddle"

Both tracks by the Cochran Brothers   —   —
          Non-album tracks

"Your Tomorrow Never Comes"   b/w "Guilty Conscience"

Both tracks by the Cochran Brothers   —   —

1955   "Walkin' Stick Boogie"   b/w "Rollin'"

Both tracks by Jerry Capeheart Featuring the Cochran Brothers   —   —

"Tired and Sleepy"   b/w "Fool's Paradise"

Both sides by the Cochran Brothers   —   —

1956   "Skinny Jim" b/w "Half Loved" —   —

1957   "Sittin' in the Balcony" b/w "Dark Lonely Street" (non-album track) 18   23   Singin' to My Baby

"Mean When I'm Mad" b/w "One Kiss" —   29

"Drive In Show"   b/w "Am I Blue" (non-album track)   82   —   Eddie Cochran

"Twenty Flight Rock" b/w "Cradle Baby" (from Singin' to My Baby) — — Never to Be Forgotten

1958   "Jeannie Jeannie Jeannie" b/w "Pocketful of Hearts"   94 —   Non-album tracks

"Teresa" b/w "Pretty Girl"   —   —

Summertime Blues" b/w "Love Again" (from Never to Be Forgotten) 8   18   Eddie Cochran

"C'mon Everybody" b/w "Don't Ever Let Me Go" (non-album track)   35   6

1959   "Teenage Heaven" b/w "I Remember" (non-album track) 99   —

"Somethin' Else" b/w "Boll Weevil Song" (from Never to Be Forgotten) 58   22

"Hallelujah I Love Her So". b/w "Little Angel" (from Never to Be Forgotten) — 22

1960 "Three Steps to Heaven" b/w "Cut Across Shorty" — 1

"Lonely" — 41 Never to Be Forgotten

"Sweetie Pie" — 38

1961 "Weekend" b/w "Lonely" (US); "Cherished Memories" (UK) — 15

The following songs also made chart entries in the UK:

1961: "Jeannie Jeannie Jeannie" - #31

1963: "My Way" - #23

1966: "Summertime Blues" - #55; #34 (1968); #53 (1975)

1988: "C'mon Everybody" - #14

1988: "Somethin' Else" - #100

A riff in search of lyrics, lyrics in search of a riff, an artist in search of identity…and Amos 'n' Andy. Put 'em together and whatta ya got? Eddie Cochran's "Summertime Blues," still the sine qua non of summer songs, after 60 years. Unlike the other summer-themed hit from 1958, the Jamies' "Summertime Summertime," a driving, doo-wop influenced paean to the joys of slipping the surly bonds of academia for fun in the sun, "Summertime Blues" suggested a darker side to the holiday, having used a hard-flailed, angry two-chord guitar riff, a thumping ostinato bass lick, and double-timed handclaps to burn its message into rock 'n' roll legend.

When Eddie co-wrote the song with his manager Jerry Capehart at Capehart's Sunset Boulevard apartment in Los Angeles during March 1958, the rocker, then only aged 17, although a professional for nearly 4 years, was going nowhere fast. He'd had a modest hit in 1957 with a version of John D. Loudermilk's "Sittin' In the Balcony," which showed that with a lot of reverb, Cochran could manage a good immitation of Elvis Presley's hiccuping vocal style and that he'd mastered Carl Perkins's razor-edged sound signature as a guitarist.

During the writing session at Capehart's apartment which he recalled in his final interview, during 1998, shortly before being diagnosed with brain cancer, of which he died on June 7th of that year, "We were looking for a hit that would give Eddie some identity." Cochran came over with his bass player, Connie "Guybo" Smith, intending to work out arrangements on 3 songs for an upcoming recording session. "We went through them all, and after we'd finished I looked at Eddie and Eddie looked at me, and he said, 'Dad, I don't think we've got anything here.'"

Capehart agreed before running an idea past Cochran: "You know, Eddie, there's never been a blues song written about the summertime. Let's write a song called 'Summertime Blues.' He then said, "Hey, I've got this new riff on the guitar,' going da-da-da-da, da-da-da-da, you know, that was the new riff. 45 minutes later it was all over–those lyrics just rolled out. Had the song as you hear it today." Asked if Cochran had written any of the lyrics, Capehart said, "He contributed a couple of words here and there. Basically I wrote the lyrics and he had the guitar lick."

Regarding the lyrics themselves, which described a young man clashing with adult authority figures - his parents, his boss at work, his Congressman - who were doing their best to keep him from living the good life of dating and driving, Capehart said he wasn't trying to cause a fuss or send a message but was seeking the Holy Grail: "We were just trying to hit the commercial market, just trying to get a hit record. As far as we were concerned, the way there was to go with basically what we were listening to on the radio. Trying to get in the pocket somewhere."

The recording session, at Gold Star Studios, which later entered legend as Phil Spector's studio of choice during the 1960s, was only intended to make a demo of the song. Capehart paid $350 for 3 hours of studio time and for a drummer sent over by the Los Angeles Musician's Union to accompany Eddie as guitarist, with Guybo Smith on bass.

Capehart couldn't recall much about the drummer–including his name–except that "he couldn't hold tempo; he was bad, so Eddie was about to go nuts. We got the one take–the one you hear on the record–everything else we had to trash. Thirty, thirty-five takes." Capehart later named New Orleans legend Earl Palmer as the drummer on all the important Cochran sessions, including "Summertime Blues.", who never had a problem holding tempo.

Eddie had a brainstorm during the recording. Capehart had written the adults' put-down lines - "I'd like to help you, son, but you're too young to vote" - intending them to be played straight. Cochran, who was given to quoting pet phrases uttered by Tim Moore's George "Kingfish" Stevens character, on the Amos 'n' Andy TV show - "His favourite expression was 'I not only resents the allegation; I resents the alligator.' That was Eddie's thing," - had the idea to do the put-down lines in Kingfish's voice. These were recorded separately then spliced into the finished track, as were the double-time handclaps coming on every other beat, courtesy of Cochran, Capehart, Smith and Gold Star engineer Larry Levine.

Levine, who died on May 8th, 2008, downplayed his role in the clean, robust sound of the finished track, which stood up to the work he did in later years with Spector, having said during 1998, "I can't take any credit for the sound other than what we had in the studio. At Gold Star we were working off spit and chewing gum. We would put things together just to make them work. Back in those days, mostly what we were using as far as microphones, and I'm sure what we used on guitar, was an Electro Voice 256. That's Eddie doing all that. The only thing I didn't do is screw it up. To me that's what a good engineer does."

Capehart was sure they'd found the elusive hit by the end of the session, Cochran having agreed, saying only, "Dad, I think we got one"–"which was a lot for him," as Capehart stated. Towards the end of his life, Eddie, long haunted by premonitions of an early death, signed autographs, "Don't forget me."

Cochran, the guy who wrote "Summertime Blues," worshipped as a deity by 21st-century rockabilly fans. Inducted into the Rock 'n' Roll Hall of Fame the second year they were open for business. Eddie was a Paradigm Guitar Player... Closer to James Marshall Hendrix than a late-1950s contemporary like James Burton, in impact. No matter in which art form, artists who've single-handedly shifted the direction of their field of artistic endeavour have been extremely rare.

There's been a small number of paradigm guitarists over the last 6 decades or so, those most often cited being Charlie Christian, Django Reinhardt, Les Paul, B.B. King, Pete Townshend, Jimi Hendrix, Eddie Van Halen... Yet, in a field that has been pored over the world over, there remained someone in the shadows, but who among the true rock cognoscenti, stood shoulder to shoulder with the all of above-mentioned... Eddie Cochran.

Cute Paul met Johnny Rhythm for the first time... c. 3:30pm on Saturday, July 6th, 1957. Paul had watched John's Quarrymen perform a few tunes at a garden party at a Liverpool church. Wanting to impress John, who was clearly the leader of the group, having just as clearly been a bit of a hard-ass, Paul knew exactly what to hit the guy with... Years later, John Lennon recalling the moment, was knocked out by the fact that Paul knew all the chords and words to "20 Flight Rock" by "everyone's idol," Eddie Cochran.

Right there, was the whole story in one word. "Idol" isn't just a word you can throw around. Eddie Cochran, the merest two-hit-wonder, also-ran in the US, his home country, was worshipped alongside Elvis Presley in Great Britain during the 1950s. Thus, among other pop-culture-stew ingredients, could the dominance of

British rock guitarists from 1964 until the early 70s be traced.

Youths learning to play the guitar in the UK towards end of the 1950s, had a big advantage, as they were paying attention to Cochran, especially the kids who'd caught his one UK tour during the Spring of 1960, which he'd just finished when he was killed in a taxi accident on his way to Heathrow to catch the plane back home for his first appearance on The Ed Sullivan Show.

Teenage boys including Jimmy Page, Pete Townshend, Ritchie Blackmore and Jeff Beck, went to see Eddie, or knew someone who did. All of them down front, where any serious guitar playing youth would be, saw something utterly new, something revolutionary. Cochran's G string was unwound, which sounds like a joke, but was one of the most pivot times in the history of the guitar. The course of popular music was to be tangibly impacted by this revelation that Eddie had brought with him from Minnesota, as word spread like wildfire.

For centuries, guitars were strung with 4 wound strings, a wire with thinner wire wound around it, and 2 plain, one wire strings, the plain strings being the highest treble strings, E and B. Normally, the 3rd string, the G, was wound, making it a tough string to bend but an unwound G makes a guitar easier to play and more expressive, with the G string usually being the one that gives the 'flavour' note in any given chord, often also being the root string when soloing.

Thus, Cochran impacted virtually every young British guitar player during the late 1950s, while American guitar kids were still sitting around waiting for The Ventures to arrive, with their straightforward and polite guitar stylings during late 1960. Eddie had been dead almost 6 months when "Walk Don't Run" was released.

Todd Rundgren, among others was producing records during the early 1970s, playing all or almost all the instruments, over-dubbing one after the other. Cochran had beaten them to that trick by well over a decade, having been the first ever rock star to write, record, produce, and play most of the instruments on his records, having done all that while still a teenager!

Eddie was only 18 during 1957, when he recorded his version of the revered "20 Flight Rock", having played all the instruments, except for his co-writer, Jerry Capehart, thumping on a cardboard carton in lieu of a snare drum. By the age of 20, Cochran had already written and recorded many of his biggest hits, several of which still stand as monuments of the highest quality and purest music produced in the infancy of Rock 'n' Roll.

Eddie was the first songwriter to adopt Chuck Berry's breakthrough observational lyric style. Cochran was a teenager, making his empathetic observations from inside the situation, rather than being the smooth, sly older man, who wrote lyrics that a Porter or Sondheim would've envied. The knowing details, laid back wit, and fully-developed vision that Eddie displayed in the lyrics of "Summertime Blues," "Somethin' Else," "Nervous Breakdown," and "Pink Peg-legged Slacks", were staggering coming from someone barely out of his teens.

Like Buddy Holly, that other true guitarist/writer/singer/producer giant of the time, Cochran was also writing using the immemorial 1 - 4 - 5 chord sequence, in ways that didn't use the the standard 1 - 4 - 1 - 5 - 4 - 1 blues sequence. Virtually every one of Eddie's masterpieces used those same 3 chords but he arranged the changes in ways that made the music new and fresh.

Cochran was blessed with looks that were in Elvis Presley's league, with his persona being much closer to Elvis's than the legendary Buddy Holly. While a deeply hard-ass, gun-carrying Texan in 'real life', Buddy presented himself as being safe as a vanilla shake. Eddie's voice, lyrics, and publicity shots, all had an authentic, brooding bad-boy quality to them, akin to James Dean.

Cochran was a wicked, years-ahead-of-his-time lead guitarist. While none of his hits had a moment where it would've made sense to cut loose, b-side and album tracks exist where he tore contemporary guys like James Burton, Scotty Moore and Link Wray to shreds. He may've also been rock 'n' roll's first-ever 'techie gearhead,' with no other photo of a modified guitar as early as Eddie's Gretsch 6120, with a Gibson P-90 pickup in the neck position being extant. Les Paul had dozens of prototypes at his disposal. Cochran was an 18-year-old youth, swapping electronics in his electric guitar during 1957, having been on the money, P-90 pick-ups being great.

Pete Townshend and Roger Daltrey were especially enamoured with Eddie's Flamenco strumming on his hit, "Three Steps To Heaven," a track that featured the strum that Townshend used to its fullest advantage in "Pinball Wizard." "Here For More", the b-side of "The Seeker," perhaps Daltrey's best songwriting effort, was really an excuse for Pete to do Eddie's "Heaven" strum every 10 seconds. Whenever Pete threw Cochran's strum into a song on stage, Roger would inevitably turn to Townshend, smiling knowingly, Pete smiling back.

Another viscerally important Cochran factor... was the big, bold chunky chug and feel of Eddie's rhythm tracks. There simply hadn't been music recorded before with the rhythmic drive and leaning-into-the-beat feel of tracks including "C'mon Everybody," "Somethin' Else,", and "Jeannie Jeannie Jeannie." Cochran's production emphasized the mid-and-low end range, thus adding an extra oomph from the bass guitar and drums. One could hear that precise feel in songs by The Who, Black Sabbath, Judas Priest, and Led Zeppelin, amongst others.

Jeff Beck released his second L.P. under the name, The Jeff Beck Group, "Beck Ola (Cosa Nostra)", featuring Rod "The Mod" Stewart on lead vocals, during the Spring of 1969, a milestone album by any critical aesthetic analysis. Having followed Jeff's first solo LP, "Truth," "Beck-Ola" was the first true blend of Flash Blues Metal and Outright Funk. Every cut was brilliant, with Jeff playing some of the wildest lead guitar ever recorded. While every track had scorching guitar throughout, there was a riff on "Hangman" that always dropped jaws. "Show me that riff. Now!"

About 5 years later, someone in Britain released the recording of the one live show Cochran performed for the BBC, just weeks before his death. Among all these great BBC performances, Eddie played his version of "Milk Cow Blues" featuring a toe curling solo. About two-thirds of the way through the song, in between vocal lines, Cochran whipped out a deadly deadly lick, complete with a psycho vibrato on the last note... Jeff Beck's transcendent "Hangman" riff... 9 years before Jeff.

Roger Daltrey announced at the Village Theater during July, 1967 that The Who were gonna do "a new one for us, but, it's an old Eddie Cochran number called 'Summertime Blues'... ." They then went into their completely over-the-top slamming version of the famous song, with the 3 chord sequence. Hunting down Cochran's albums in New York back then was almost impossible, decades before all the videos of Eddie Cochran appeared on YouTube. Much of the music you really like, sounds the way it does because of a teenage guitarist who delivered the musical gifts of a lifetime then "left the building" nearly 6 months before his 22nd birthday.

The driver lost control and hit a lamp post as they entered Chippenham, 14 miles northeast of Bath. Sitting alongside his girlfriend and songwriter Sharon Sheeley, who had just turned 20, and fellow rocker Gene Vincent, who was asleep, Cochran had repeatedly asked the driver to slow down. The section of the A4 between Bath and Chippenham is pretty tortuous in parts.

Eddie had enough time to shield Sheeley as the car crashed and threw its passengers out onto the road. Sharon recalled later that as she and the unconscious Cochran were loaded into the ambulance, the thoughtful medic clasped the lovers' hands for their last ride together. They were transferred to St. Martin's Hospital where he died of severe head injuries about 4 p.m. It was Easter Sunday. Ritchie Valens' mother, attended the funeral.

For some rock stars who found fame and fortune much later, the '50s might have been the high point of rock 'n' roll. Tom Petty recalled in a 2009 Rolling Stone interview how he and fellow Travelling Wilbury George Harrison shared an obsession with '50s music, having wryly noted, "With George, I think his interest in rock waned around 1962."

Mick Jagger, who was 16 when Eddie Cochran died, was a huge fan. "The cat is royalty, man," he told Pittsburgh radio program director John Rook during 1964. About 40 years later Jagger recalled, "On the records, his sound was really fantastic. They sound very crystal clear, with a good use of sound in itself—beautifully recorded, produced records … They happened to be very influential on all British bands coming up in the '60s, and still even now these records are known to British musicians." The Stones covered Cochran's "Twenty Flight Rock" on their 1981 tour.

While Cochran made Britain aware of American rock n'roll, his contribution there did much to introduce the world to the British invasion of the Beatles and a host of other legendary UK recording stars. George Harrison, John Lennon, Paul McCartney, Cliff Richard and many others credited Eddie with having helped to motivate them to achieve stardom.

A billboard displaying Hollywood's newest blonde bombshell Jayne Mansfield with Tom Ewell in the background promoted "The Girl Can't Help It". The new comedy was obviously trading on the recent success of Hollywood's top sex symbol Marilyn Monroe, who's "Seven Year Itch" also with Tom Ewell, had been a major box office hit.

Hollywood was awash in blonde sex kittens. Big band leader Ray Anthony's wife, Mamie Van Doren, Kim Novak and an immensely endowed sexpot from Sweden, Anita Ekberg, were among the Marilyn hopefuls, ready to claim a title that had been vacant since the platinum blonde locks of Jean Harlow had hit the screen two decades earlier. "The Girl Can't Help It" was already playing in cinemas, with Jayne Mansfield, advertised as being even sexier than Marilyn.

The hype on the lot included Eddie Cochran, who was prominently displayed on the poster promoting the movie. Gene Vincent and his Blue Caps and Little Richard, were also in the picture, the latter having many fans, including listeners of the Hunter Hancock radio show.

Eddie Cochran's version of Twenty Flight Rock" was being played on a small speaker in the waiting room. The word "black" hadn't yet surfaced in describing negro artists, but the crossover of "race" music was beginning to find acceptance as white America discovered it via the radio.

"Twenty Flight Rock" sounded wild, making one want to know more about its originator, Eddie Cochran. The world hadn't yet heard of the Beatles, of Lennon and McCartney or George Harrison, but they'd experience the same excitement upon hearing this singer. Both George Harrison and John Lennon would tell of how Eddie had influenced their lives, a decade or more in the future.

Trying to make contact with Eddie Cochran, asking if he was also a student at the Pasadena Playhouse, produced the response "yes, he could be", it being suggested one could leave a note at the studio message centre for him. A makeshift letter was scribbled, suggesting that if Eddie was attending the playhouse they could share a ride to classes there.

Heading west down Santa Monica Boulevard, on the radio KMPC's Johnny Grant introduced Sittin' in the Balcony" by Eddie Cochran. Surely this singer wasn't the same as had been heard singing "Twenty Flight Rock"? Turning up the volume, his voice sounded more like Dean Martin than a rocker.

Less than than a week later, a telephone call was received from Eddie's mother, Alice Cochran, with an invitation to meet Eddie at his home in Bell Gardens, south of Los Angeles. Explaining that he'd been spending long hours in the studio, sometimes not getting home until sunrise, she suggested a visit at 11am the following Saturday.

The Cochran's house was a light greenish/yellow, with big shade trees on a corner lot. Stepping up to the large cement slab entrance area, the door partially cracked open, with a diminutive lady's glasses peering through the opening, holding a finger to her lips…sshhh, "He's not up yet", she smiled. She opened the door wider, saying, "Oh no, come on in, he'll be up pretty soon, I'm sure".

Entering, she turned to a much larger lady, who extended her hand in welcome, saying, "I'm Gloria, Eddie's sister" and hanging on to Gloria, a preschool sized, red headed little boy was introduced as "little Ed". Mrs. Cochran offered her own hand to shake saying, "He's Gloria's boy and I'm Eddie's mom, Alice."

She motioned toward the living room couch saying, "Have a seat, tell me all about yourself, where are you from, when is your birthday, your favourite food, what kind of music do you like"? In rapid fire, a friendly grilling being delivered, before getting an introduction to her son. Both she and Gloria smiled approvingly with each answer, "You're a Libra, when were you born, what date?" October 9th, a glance to Gloria, arching her eyebrows saying, "On my!".

Someone in a white house robe at the kitchen stove was pouring coffee. Looking in the same direction Alice said, "Eddie's up," as he entered the room carrying a cup, pausing to take a sip before offering his hand in welcome. Alice interrupted, "Eddie this is Johnnie Rook" and you'll never guess when his birthday is". "Same as mine?" he guessed.

"Close, his is on the 9th and he loves cornbread and beans" she laughed and continued, "Eddie was born on October 3rd and his favourite is cornbread and beans too". Patting his unruly, uncombed hair down on his head and reaching for a cigarette to light, he said in a surprisingly deep voice, "Well that's a start".

Eddie was several inches shorter than Johnnie, with his voice sounding as though he was just getting over a bad cold. Clearing it, he blamed the hoarseness on many hours of recent studio work. Gloria added, "Yes but he loves it, he'd rather be there than almost anywhere". Alice corrected, "'cept maybe the desert, huh honey", as he half-heartedly nodded in agreement. Gloria asked, "Have you been up there?" "Up where"? Johnnie replied.

Eddie chimed in, "Nope I reckin' he ain't been there yet"? All 3 began to educate Johnnie on the beauty of the southern California desert as he answered that he'd always thought the desert was just sand and sun. Taking another sip of coffee, Eddie stood then pointing his cup toward the kitchen motioned Johnnie to follow him into his bedroom. As they passed through the kitchen he glanced at a stack of clean coffee cups in a draining rack, saying "Grab some coffee man?". "No thanks, I've already had my quota for the day", Johnnie replied.

The window blinds were still drawn blotting out the daylight, Rook adjusting his vision as Cochran motioned Johnnie to join him in sitting on the edge of his bed. Eddie leaned forward to pull a folding chair with a tape recorder sitting hap-hazardly on it then began rapidly rewinding a tape, saying it was the fruit of his endeavours from the previous night's studio work.

"See what ya think of this," Cochran said, as he propped himself up against a pillow resting against the bed's headboard, inhaling another deep hit from his cigarette. Johnnie's attention was glued to the contents on the tape, as Eddie stared at him, waiting for a response. After listening to 4 selections he reached to stop the tape recorder asking, "What da you think man?"

Johnnie gave a positive reaction to 3 of the selections, before Eddie interrupted, "How 'bout the second cut?"" Johnnie replied that he liked the instrumental but it didn't grab him like the other 3. Eddie smiled then for the first time Rook heard what was to become a familiar part of Eddie Cochran, his Amos and Andy impressions. "I don't know brotha, but I think yer right". Standing up, Eddie shook his cigarette pack at Johnnie, "Smoke? he said, "Sure," Rook answered, as Cochran clicked his lighter to fire up Johnnie's 'fag'.

Alice entered the room with a coffee pot, as Eddie leaned toward her, extending his cup for a refill. "Morning fuel", he said with a smile as Alice turned to

Rook saying, "Did you want some Johnnie". Before Cochran could answer Rook said, "Sure", as Alice turned, returning to the kitchen for a cup then Eddie looked at him challenging, "You think Shrimpers coffee is better than mine?" "Shrimper". Johnnie questioned, "Yeh, that's her given name, her real name is mama".

Reentering the bedroom carrying a cup for Rook, Alice added, "Whose given name?" grinning in delight Eddie replied, "Why yer's mama". "And who gave it to me darling?" asked Alice. "You're looking at him mama," said Eddie, prompting Alice to reach out enveloping him in a hug.

Changing into street clothes Cochran said he needed to replace a broken guitar string then Johnnie suggested they take his car, Eddie agreeing, surprising him by saying "I don't drive man". It was only a short distance to the Bell Gardens Music Center, where they were greeted by the lone clerk, "Hey Ed'erd, how ya doin'"" then again the Amos in Eddie came from his mouth, "Doin' jes fine Kingfish". It was obvious Cochran was a regular, as he went about helping himself.

Returning to his house Eddie asked about Johnnie's work week and did it allow Rook to join him the following week at the studio. Explaining he had two days free, Cochran gave Johnnie directions to Liberty records on LaBrea Ave. in Hollywood, right across from Big Tiny Naylor's drive inn restaurant.

They pulled up in front of the house in time for Cochran to introduce Rook to Gloria's husband, Red Julson, who was busy tidying up his traveling lunch wagon truck that supplied sandwiches, soup, soft drinks and chocolate bars to hungry factory workers on their break. As Eddie began to help empty some of the water from the melting ice trays into the gutter of the curb, he spilled some of the contents on himself, creating a wet spot starting just below his waist and down his pant leg.

Red broke into a broad smile with Cochran's disgust registering as he attempted to brush some of the wetness away, before heading to the front door of the house. Rushing past his mother in the kitchen on his way to his bedroom he said, "Sorry Shrimper, I just couldn't hold it!""

Alice caught on immediately, feigning a look of horror, with her eyes widening and her mouth dropping open in disbelief. Johnnie began to understand the game she and Eddie would play in their very special relationship, with Shrimper on the receiving end of his humour and loving every minute of it.

Besides Eddie, the Cochran residence was home to Gloria, Red and their son 'Little Ed', as well as Eddie's mother and father, Frank and Alice. Eddie was treated like royalty by his mother and sister as they handled his fan mail, while trying to attend his every wish.
Eddie was the pride of the ladies in the house but both Frank and Red seemed slightly envious of the special treatment he received. However, it wasn't something they could discuss within ear-shot of Alice or Gloria.

Returning from work, Frank, would set his empty lunch box on the kitchen counter then slowly pass through the living room on his way to his bedroom, where he stayed until called to dinner. He was a quiet man, withdrawn from the family, rarely commenting on anything, seemingly bored with his life, having decided it was best to keep quiet around the women in the family.

When Red wasn't selling snacks to hungry factory workers from the back of his truck, he was parked in front of the Cochran's home, stocking and cleaning the traveling lunch wagon, preparing it for the next day's run. He'd comment on Eddie's inability to make a financial contribution to the family's expenses, his remarks usually being aimed at Eddie's manager, Jerry Capehart, who Red had little time for, not being able to understand why Eddie's career wasn't paying off more.

"When's all of this gonna mean something" he'd say, as Gloria would glare disapprovingly at him, little of his discontent reaching Eddie's ears. Johnnie liked Red, who always made him feel welcome, while doing what he could to make Eddie's life better.

Red and Gloria's son, Little Ed, was a shy pre-schoolboy, who adored his uncle. Eddie would chase his red headed little nephew around the back of the house, where the wee boy would pretend to hide in a basement stairwell, with Eddie playfully hunting him down, pretending his out-stretched pointing finger was the barrel of a gun, shooting Little Ed, then blowing the smoke from the barrel exclaiming, "Gotcha!"

On Rook's first visit to the Cochran home, Alice asked, "You're gonna be staying for dinner with us aren't ya Johnnie"? Eddie answered for him, "Yes he is", as he entered the kitchen from his bedroom wearing dry slacks. Even without Johnnie, the Cochran breakfast nock would have been a snug fit for the family.

Eddie and Johnnie filled their plates then headed for his bedroom to eat then listen to a new Marty Robbins album. Having been brought up on "western music" as it was then called, they started with 'I Walk the Line'" and 'Hey Porter!' by Johnny Cash, before listening to

"Young Blood" by the Coasters, which Eddie really liked as he sang along,

"I saw her standin' on the corner, A yellow ribbon in her hair, I couldn't stop myself from shoutin', Look a-there! Look a-there! Look a-there!"

He emphasized the "Look a-there, Look a-there!" Little Richard was next, "I hear ya knockin' but you can't come in!" Eddie sang along, saying more than once, "That's the best rock band in the business!" Fats Domino wasn't far behind in Eddie's admiration. Johnnie asked Eddie what he thought of Elvis, "He's the cat man", he replied. Johnnie said he'd seen Elvis in Long Beach, during his first appearance in California, but Eddie corrected him, "The Shrine was his first stop then Long Beach". It was the only time they ever spoke of Elvis. However, in the future Elvis and Johnnie talked at length about Eddie.

Hearing the name Elvis, Alice entered the bedroom asking, "Did I hear that naughty word in here?" Eddie smiled then with a shake of his head answered, "Now Shrimper, that's uncalled for," but Rook was sure Eddie had nothing but admiration for Elvis. "Beans and cornbread next weekend Johnnie?" she baited him as Rook looked at Eddie shaking his head then replied, "I'll be here!".

Thinking it was about time for him to head home to Santa Monica, Johnnie stood then stretched as Eddie lit up another cigarette, following him to the living room with Alice interrupting his departure, saying "Sit for awhile", motioning to the couch. Rook said how much he'd enjoyed their hospitality, as Alice began to explain Eddie's early career.

"He learned to play guitar all by himself. His older brother Bill gave him his first guitar," Eddie interrupting, "Don't forget Bob!". Alice continued, "Well yes honey, Bob did teach you some chords, but you did most of it yourself". Thinking that Hank Cochran was another son, Johnnie asked, "What about Hank?", but as a smile of dismissal came on her face Alice explained, "Hank isn't related, he just had the same surname and was quite a bit older than Eddie". Breaking into a giggle she added, "They sure covered the ground together though", as she looked at Eddie, who didn't bother to respond.

Hank Cochran, became famed as an excellent song writer during the years ahead. Eddie had dropped out of high school and toured California, Oregon, Washington, Arizona then into the Midwest and South into Texas with Hank, playing as the Cochran Brothers. Hank had done most of the vocals, with Eddie on lead guitar, while singing harmony. "'Cause his voice was changing", said Gloria. Not missing a beat, Alice said, "Well he really got some of his first experience right here, at the American Legion". "Where he and Bob Bull played"," Gloria added.

An embarrassed grin came on Eddie's face as he stood and motioned Johnnie toward the front door, "That's enough!" he said. Alice couldn't stop, her eyes twinkling in pride, daring Rook to answer, "Now tell me Johnnie, who's best, Elvis or Eddie?" More embarrassment for Eddie, as he pushed Johnnie through the door to the outside then they walked to Rook's car, parked on the side street alongside the house.

Johnnie turned to shake hands as Cochran repeated the directions to Liberty Records, where they'd meet again during the week. Rook reached to his shirt pocket for a cigarette then bid goodbye to his new friend, as Eddie continued, "It's a light grey stucco building". Johnnie nodded then started the car, turning on the radio with Chuck Berry's 'School Day'," prompting Eddie to join in, "Dropped the coin right into the slot!" he sang as Rook slowly drove away smiling.

Pulling up to park in the small Liberty lot Johnnie could see Eddie standing on an outside entrance to the 2nd floor of the building, on a fire escape. He motioned for Rook to take the short cut, not bothering to enter through the main entrance. Taking steps two at a time Johnnie reached the top as Cochran greeted him, "Howdy Andy", in his best Amos and Andy imitation.

Pressing his hand to Rook's back, ushering him into the hallway of the studio, Eddie then turned to wave at two guys arriving in the parking lot below. "That's Don and Phil" he said, motioning for them to follow Johnnie's path up the fire escape. He walked ahead inside to view the studio, with 3 or 4 musicians behind the large glass window, turning toward Eddie, as he introduced Rook to the Everly Brothers. The 3 of them chatted for a few minutes, before Eddie excused himself then they left down the same staircase to the parking lot below.

As Johnnie walked into the control room, Cochran continued into the studio then through the microphone introduced Rook to Jerry Capehart, who was sitting behind the control board, "Jerry, say hello to Johnnie Rook". Shaking hands with Jerry, who rose from his chair slightly, the second guy behind the board nodded then introduced himself, "Hi, I'm Ted".

Picking up his guitar from a stand in the studio, Eddie practiced a riff or two then looking at the others, began to count down "a one, a two", as the studio musicians joined in, with Cochran beginning to sing "Let me tell ya bout a girl I know", the Ray Charles classic picked to be a cut on his L.P. "Singing to my Baby". Eddie stopped abruptly then looking through the studio glass at Capehart said, "That'll be fine man, with some sweetening". Jerry answered, "Yeh the fiddles will make it".

Several minutes went by, with Eddie running through some riffs on his guitar before stopping to take a swallow from a whiskey bottle. Letting the ingredients trickle down his throat, which Johnnie later learned was a mixture of honey and whiskey, used to sooth his strained vocal chords.

He again began to pick some chords on his guitar, then turning to the bass player asked, "Ready Connie"? as they begin to play together. Rook later met Connie Smith at the Cochran home, where in introducing him as "Guybo", Eddie would add humorously, "or Connie Smith if you're the law!". This session would be to record "Tell me Why" and as he strained to hit the high notes he stopped, with a wink to Johnnie, before taking another swig from the bottle. Looking again at Rook he said, "Medicine!" with a grin.

Eddie's star was beginning to shine brighter, but not bright enough financially. Sy Warnoker, Liberty's owner, allowed Cochran to get record in experience in the studio when it wasn't in use but promotion was still required for radio airplay. Liberty Records was a struggling little label, with hardly any of the muscle Elvis's RCA records had.

Johnnie offered to drop out of his Playhouse classes, to go on the road promoting Eddie's records but he said no, until after 3 unsuccessful releases, he agreed. While

Cochran believed the material Liberty was giving him to record was sub-standard, Jerry Capehart encouraged him to continue to record it.

Johnnie returned from a fortnight on the road to hear Eddie and Jerry arguing over material, Cochran insisting that he could create better songs than those the label had given him to record, also wanting to record from a different studio than the one at Liberty. Jerry finally agreed then they began to use the studio at Gold Star.

Johnnie could see a much more confident Eddie emerge from those sessions, as he began to find a niche that he was more comfortable with. He began not only to play guitar, but experiment with other sounds, like using a card board box for a drum and to get a special effect he began to do what he called overdub himself. Rook went to work at Liberty, packing boxes of records for shipping to DJs across the country.

It wasn't long before Cochran's studio experimentation started to lead him in a new direction, as he began using studio B at Gold Star exclusively. The run down little studio off Santa Monica boulevard and Vine in Hollywood, was a real favourite for Eddie. It would be where most of his music would be created, including the classic, "Summertime Blues".

Gold Star might not have been as classy as the big major studios in town, but soon it became known as where most of the rockers wanted to record. Many artists would ask for Cochran to be included in their sessions, who was happiest in the studio. Years later, Johnnie would grimace when finding out that the historic Gold Star studio had been torn down to make way for a mini mall, the recording studio used by more artists than any other being destroyed without a word of complaint.

"Let's go to lunch Rookie", Ross Badisariun tempted Johnnie to end his sweaty morning packing discs at Liberty Records. Ross recorded under the name of David Seville, creator of the Chipmunks, Rook counting him as a good friend in those early days. His wee jazz band recorded "Armen's Theme" with modest success and he was a part time actor and songwriter, who had many helpful contacts in the movie business.

The lunch invitation was well received by the hungry Johnnie, it always having been a pleasure having Ross as his host, whose taste in restaurants was excellent. Entering the El Dorado in Hollywood, Badisariun tabled hopped twice, dispensing the usual shop talk then at Tennessee Ernie Fords table, accepted an invitation to join him.

Rook was impressed and captivated by the ole pea-picker's southern drawl and country charm. Having grown up a fan of Tennessee Ernie's, Johnnie found his charisma magnetic, not just for him but everyone in the restaurant. In his wildest dreams Rook would never have guessed that he'd become the person most responsible for his future.

Asking Johnnie "What's your game young man", Ross interrupted saying he was an up and coming actor. Next question, "Are you a dedicated actor, or just exploring?" Rook answered that so far it hadn't taken him by storm then as he began to explain why, Tennessee interrupted, suggesting a career in radio would be his choice if he were a young man again.

He said how many radio announcers of the day were transferring their talents to TV, predicting hundreds of new radio stations would be added to the dial in the near future, creating a shortage of announcers. Johnnie could hardly keep his mind on anything else for the remainder of their lunch, as his advice had sparked his excitement.

Bitten by the radio bug, Rook began listening more to the voices of Joe Yokum, Earl McDaniel, Art LaBoe, Art Way, Peter Potter & Johnny Grant. He'd repeat and improve on the patter they delivered between the records. Johnnie began creating ads to read from the newspaper, fantasizing of being a DJ on KLAC, KMPC and the Mighty 690.

On one of their desert outings Rook told Cochran of his hopes of becoming a DJ, seeing a frown of disbelief, as Eddie wasn't at first overly convinced. Later though he'd agree, but reminded Johnnie of the painful fact that he'd have to get some experience elsewhere than Los Angeles. Took really liked California, so it would take some time for him to imagine leaving the exciting paradise for a boring life in some distant town.

However, Rook also knew that he had some serious misgivings about pursuing a career as an actor. It just didn't move fast enough for his tastes, while radio was immediate, and all he could think of was how fine it would be hearing that great music, while getting paid for it.

Ernie Ford's suggestion was with Johnnie day and night, even in his sleep he dreamed of being a DJ. The lure finally led Rook to bite the bullet then begin looking for a job in radio in California. Almost immediately, Johnnie could see that Eddie was right, without a tape and a resume documenting his experience, no doors cracked, let alone opened in Los Angeles.

A few months later Cochran expressed his frustration over an upcoming tour of Australia. He was booked to join Little Richard, Gene Vincent & Bill Haley, introducing rock 'n' roll down under. Commercial jets had yet to become part of the TWA air fleet, with the much slower prop driven planes having made for a long, long trip, of at least 20 hours flying time, almost all over the waters of the Pacific Ocean.

Having toured for several years already of his young lifetime, Eddie always grew depressed when approaching a trip, especially traveling so far away from home. He loved home, so would've been happy just spending time in the studio experimenting with recording techniques. He'd already been recognized by many experts as being a leading guitar player, with his "overdubbing" recording being considered revolutionary in an industry still in its infancy.

Eddie had telephoned saying 'We have to go to the desert before I have to live out of that damn suitcase again'. Capehart had scheduled him to join the Biggest Show of Stars for 1957, straight after returning from the exhausting Australian trip. In an attempt to cheer him up and take his mind off the upcoming torture of the Aussie tour, they headed to Hesperia and the desert. Bob Bull, who recorded as Bob Denton on Dot Records, Eddie and Johnnie behind the wheel, paid tribute to Fats Domino's

"Sick 'n' Tired. Oo Baby, Whatcha Gonna Do", singing at the top of their voices.

Cochran's staples for a trip to the desert were beer, cigarettes, whiskey, his long barrel six shooter and a friend or two, being all he needed for a good time. Eddie seldom wore Levis except on these desert trips. A

Levi jacket and his beat up cowboy hat topped-off the fashion statement for the outings.

This particular desert trip was remembered as the one when Eddie went hunting, or was it rustling? As usual Johnnie was driving, Bob was in the back seat and Cochran was, as he would say, "Ridin' shotgun" in the front passenger seat. As the driver Johnnie laid off the alcohol, except for a beer or two.

Rook never witnessed Eddie ever drinking at home, but during times at leisure, away from his family, he had an amazing ability to consume beer. It wasn't unusual for him to sink a dozen cans during one hot afternoon on the desert, really being semi-desert, having sage brush, a tree or two wherever they could survive and some giant boulders here and there.

As Johnnie drove along with the car radio blasting away, suddenly Cochran yelled, "Whoa Andy, stop this wagon!". Screeching to a halt, Eddie ordered, "Back this stage up to that rock back there". Rook thought it was a stop to release some of the liquid he'd swallowed, so he and Bob stayed in the car as Cochran opened the door with his pistol in hand then left their vision behind a giant boulder.

A few minutes later over the sound of the radio Bob and Johnnie were startled to hear the sound of gunshots...two of them, from where Eddie had disappeared. Fear raced through them as they hurried from the car, just in time to see Cochran coming from behind the boulder, blowing the smoke from his pistol's barrel, with a grin on his face saying, "I think ol' Ed'erd jest got us some beef boys".

He explained during the release of his body fluid that he'd been startled by a yearling steer and "for my own safety boys, I had to protect myself!". Leading them to the carcass, Eddie persuaded them that it'd be a shame to waste all that beef, instructing Johnnie to return to the car then prepare the boot for loading and transporting his prize to his brother Bob's house.

Steak and hamburger was plentiful that autumn and winter in Bob Cochran's home but one must pay for such actions. Johnnie didn't know for many years but Eddie's nephew, Bobby Cochran later told him that the carcass had to be dug up from his backyard then moved to a distant burial site, as the summer heat released a terrible stench, due to it having been buried too shallow. Johnnie kept quiet about the hunting trip, not mentioning it to his mother until at least a dozen years after Cochran's death. Her surprised response was, "Oh Johnnie, you kids! How could you let him do that?". Eddie could still do no wrong to her way of thinking.

Drugs were not a part of their lives during the 50's, their behavior having been tame compared with later teens activities. They did have strip poker parties with giggling young ladies eager to lose hand after hand to Eddie, who was seldom forced to discard more than his boots. Cochran was always a gentleman, seldom using profanity, having been a magnet for young females.

Johnnie decided to sell his car for $180, to get the money he'd need to move to begin his new career in radio. He decided to travel by Trailways bus lines instead of Greyhound because it was cheaper. Having announced his plans, Alice phoned Rook asking him to come to dinner, saying she was planning "yours and Eddie's favourite meal", as a send off for both of them,

Johnnie heading east, to points unknown and Eddie west on his Australian tour.

Thinking he'd be lucky enough to find employment in Salt Lake City Rook said that he didn't expect to be that far away and after a short period gaining experience, would return to southern California. "Well, just the same, you better come and see Eddie before you both leave", replied Alice.

The weather was hot during late summer, so sweat was pouring off of Eddie's sister Gloria, as she stood ironing shirts in the kitchen, preparing for his Australian departure. Alice was in his bedroom packing Cochran's suitcase as Johnnie arrived late in the afternoon. Eddie wasn't home but was expected to return soon from the Bell Gardens Music Center, where he'd gone to pick up some extra strings for his guitar.

Alice's smile of welcome turned into a worrisome frown as she hugged Took, saying, "Its not easy Johnnie", as she registered her concern over Eddie leaving on a trip that would take him "half way around the world". Her lips tightened then tears came to her eyes as she excused herself with a nervous laugh, saying, "I'm just a worry wart!". Gloria nodded her head in agreement then handed Alice a freshly ironed shirt to be packed.

Eddie's mother complained that he wouldn't be home for his 19th birthday but at least they could celebrate their birthdays together, his on the 3rd and Johnnie's on the 9th of October. He'd be catching a flight out of LAX the following day. Alice apologized for not being able to serve the promised beans and cornbread but Gloria said a dinner of fried chicken should satisfy them somewhat. Entering the front door with his brother in law Red,

Eddie gave his usual greeting, "Howdy dere' Andy", as Red offered a handshake.

Complaining about Eddie's upcoming schedule, Red brought a silence to the room, as he blamed Jerry Capehart for Cochran having to join a tour of the US shortly after returning from Australia. "Jerry doesn't give a damn, he doesn't have to go!", said Red, as Gloria stared disapprovingly in his direction.

Attempting to put a positive face on this trip, Eddie seemed in good spirits when in the company of his mother and Gloria, but as Johnnie was about to leave for his home, with an expression of exasperation on his face, he said, "straight ahead man, I'll see ya, I just don't know when".

Three days later Rook was climbing the steps to the second floor offices of KALL in downtown Salt Lake City, hoping to impress the program director, "Daddy Flo" so that he'd be given his first job in radio. He listened to Johnnie's energetic pitch, but said he'd need experience in a smaller market. He knew of no openings anywhere but suggested Rook try Denver, where he said several top 30 radio stations were located.

Johnnie hurried to the depot to catch a late afternoon bus east to Denver, where the program director at KIMN, Grahame Richards, was regarded as one of the nation's innovators of top 30 radio. He was cordial but again Rook got the same suggestion, gain experience in a smaller market but keep him informed of his growth in the business, because he was creating several pop music radio stations in distant cities.

Richards aimed Johnnie in the direction of Scottsbluff, Nebraska where he'd been told of an opening at KOLT.

Arriving in Scottsbluff late at night, Rook slept on a bus station bench then waited for the program director to arrive late the following morning. Sitting in the lobby of the station waiting, the receptionist told Johnnie the job had been filled two days earlier then the program director had called in sick, so wouldn't be at the station until the following Monday. It being a Friday, Rook decided not to waste what few dollars he had left then after telephoning KNEB, being told they had no openings, decided to catch a bus to return home to Chadron, a hundred miles north.

Arriving in Chadron unexpectedly on an early Saturday morning, Johnnie walked the 15 blocks to his parent's home, where his mother Della was delighted to see him, despite being awaken by his ring of the doorbell. Johnnie's father wasn't that pleased, telling him that very afternoon "Don't think you're going to lay around here living off me".

As Rook began to say that he was going to try for a career in radio, his father ridiculed him, saying that it was ridiculous and Johnnie should consider something more suitable, like a job greasing steam locomotives at his place of employment, the C&NW railroad. However, he cautioned, "I doubt they'll even let you join the union, do you have any money for the entrance fee"? Attempting to cool Johnnie down, his mother Della interrupted to ask if he wanted to go grocery shopping with her.

Checking in with the local radio station, KCSR, his DJ friend there, Freeman Hover, told Rook about a possible opening at KASL in New Castle, Wyoming. Telephoning the station, Johnnie was advised they did have an opening but if he was interested he should make the more than 100 mile drive to apply promptly, as they had several applicants and would be making a decision within a few days.

Ten days after departing Los Angeles, Rook got his first job in radio at KASL. The station offered programming to the 2,000 citizens of New Castle and about 30 miles of range land, with all its cattle. Roy Marsh, the manager of the station suggested Johnnie stand behind him in the studio for a day, before taking to the airwaves himself. Rook assured him he had some limited experience, when truthfully he'd never been on the air before.

Johnnie recalled hearing him introduce the midday housewife program just once then for the next several months repeated the same introduction, "It's 10 am and transcribed, time for ladylendanear...", leading into the next musical selection, that came from an old world disc, a 3 ft wide red vinyl record that required the needle be placed on the inside groove to start, just the opposite of a regular phonograph recording.

These discs needed their own turntable, a heavy cast iron contraption with wheels, allowing it to be moved to a location nearer the control board. Johnnie hated what they played, very tinny sounding music from the 1930's and 40's, from orchestras of that era. Embarrassingly, after several weeks, Rook discovered the name of the midday show was not, ladylendanear , but "Lady lend an ear". .

Johnnie arrived at work to began his announcing duties at 9am then worked until
10pm, 6 days a week. He looked forward to the 8pm to 10pm House of Wax program, when he was allowed to play the rock hits from the Billboard top 30. Race music hadn't yet made it to all white Wyoming. Even if it had,

they received very few records from the small record companies that distributed that music. Elvis was permitted but Little Richard covers by Pat Boone were the versions aired in the farm and ranch areas of America.

Eddie called while on tour from Cincinnati, Ohio, while traveling in a crowded bus, being exhausted. He said that while on the plane flying over the Pacific, Little Richard had a conversion, having announced that he was giving up rock n' roll to preach the gospel.
That had upset Eddie, as he really liked Little Richard's music and while he had no problem with Richard entering the ministry, he would sorely miss his musical contribution. He wondered what would happen to Little Richard's band, chuckling as he announced, "Ladys and Gentlemen, it's Eddie Cochran with Little Richard's band". Johnnie said, "No, yer kiddin!" as he laughed.

Within 6 months, Rook learned a new more powerful radio station would be broadcasting from Hot Springs, South Dakota. Moving from KASL to KOBH would mean an increase of $10 / week. $80 / week and reduced hours, from 6am til' 6pm, allowed Johnnie to have some nightlife. It wasn't California, but located in the foothills of the Black Hills, with the influx of tourism in the summer months, Hot Springs was a happening place.

However, Rook soon found out that opening up the station at 6am meant he'd have to arrive in enough time to prepare a full 10 minute newscast to begin the broadcast day. Also, to ready the station's broadcast transmitter, the filaments needed a full 20 minutes of warm up time, before broadcasting.

With Johnnie's alarm going off at 4am then a 5am arrival at the station, it wasn't long before he discovered his nightlife wasn't all he'd hoped for. Work laws and unions were unheard of for smalltown radio stations, so upon finding out he wouldn't be paid for the time it took him to prepare was a disappointment. Rook would always think of his first hour at work as a free hour.

Jim Reeves was a big favorite with the station manager when he stopped by to be interviewed and in response to Johnnie quizzing him about the new rock n' roll music, said, "Everyone to their own poison". Patsy Cline visited with a tape of her singing "Sweet Dreams" asking if he'd play it so she could hear it on her car radio while heading north to Rapid City, saying it'd be a great way for her to judge the mix of the song, to hear how it would sound coming from a radio speaker.

Al Martino, Connie Francis, Brenda Lee, Jimmy Jones and Paul Anka phoned to be interviewed on the air and Eddie Cochran phoned to see how Rook's new career was going, having been interviewed twice on the air. KOBH was at 580 on the dial being heard in at least 5 states. Eddie had asked why he didn't change his broadcasting name to a more believable Johnnie Rowe, as by doing so he'd no longer have to explain the last name of Rho.

The station attracted a large audience, with the Hooper ratings showing it got 58% of the listening audience in the Black Hills area. Johnnie spent 3 weeks broadcasting daily from a platform anchored on top of telephone polls, raising money for the Brainard Indian School. A goal of $30,000 was reached before he was allowed to come down from his perch after more than a fortnight, with a sleeping bag and a tent for shelter. Food traveled up to Rook via a pulley rope, his only communication coming from a phone and a microphone extension to the studio for broadcasting.

Johnnie lived in a rental one bedroom mobile home in a trailer park. It was a cold snowy day during early February 1959 when Alice Cochran phoned to ask if he could fly out to be with Eddie, who was deeply depressed, mourning the death of his good friend Buddy Holly. A single engine plane with Buddy, Richie Valens and J.P. Richardson, known as the Big Bopper, had crashed just a few miles outside of Mason City, Iowa.

They were part of a tour, traveling by bus, which had kept breaking down, so they'd decided to rent a small plane to fly them ahead, to get to their next venue with enough time for them to get some much needed rest before their next show. The tragedy hit Eddie especially hard, as he and Buddy had formed a strong friendship during their Australian tour the previous year.

Johnnie soon left for Rapid City to catch a flight to Denver then on to California. Red Julson picked him up at Los Angeles airport then as they drove to the Cochran house in silence Rook only remembered him saying, "Eddie's pretty torn up Johnnie". It was a gloomy visit to the Cochran home, not at all like the fun filled days of the past. Alice met Rook at the door then without saying anything reached up to give him a hug and a kiss before he entered the house.

She shook her head in distress, with tears in her eyes then as they walked into the living room Eddie appeared from his bedroom, offering a combined handshake and hug saying "Good to see ya man". They walked silently into his bedroom then as Johnnie stared out of the window at the outside world, Eddie picked up his guitar, beginning to quietly pick on the strings with a pained frown on his face.

After several minutes, Eddie was standing behind Johnnie, reaching for his shoulders to turn Rook around to face him then said, "if anything like this happens to me, promise me you'll take care of Shrimper," Ok? Johnnie assured him he would, later honouring that pledge for the more than 30 years remaining of her life.

Alice poked her head in the bedroom door to ask if Rook was hungry then as he answered he wasn't, Eddie laid his guitar down on the bed before motioning for Johnnie to follow him outside. It was pleasant feeling the warmth of the California sun but a cloud clearly shadowed Eddie's mind as he stopped to gaze blindly at some flowers. His back was turned to Rook but he could see Eddie was quietly crying. As Johnnie approached him then placed an arm around his neck he turned away, wiping the tears from his face with his hand.

That evening Bob Cochran arrived, Johnnie noticing an improvement in Eddie's mood as he embraced and smiled at seeing his much loved brother. Bob looked at Rook saying, "How you been disc jockey John". It was the first time Johnnie had seen Bob since the change in his career, Eddie having picked up on the theme remarking "Disc Jockey John ain't playin' enough Eddie Cochran records". The humour was a welcome relief, so Rook thought he'd help it along by saying that he only played the hits. Bob responded, "Your job is to make them hits boy!".

Coming from another area of the house, sister Gloria interrupted, asking how Johnnie's flight was, which prompted Eddie to add, "Flight, I didn't know they had airplanes out there in Indian country!". Rook didn't recall seeing Frank during this visit but thought it was on this trip that he'd met Eddie's sister Pat and her husband Hank, as they stopped by briefly.

Johnnie thought his arrival had broken some of the gloom that had brought him to the Cochran home, as after two days Alice managed a smile as he said it was time for him to return to South Dakota. Tears came to her eyes as he hugged her before Eddie said goodbye then Red took him to the airport for the return trip home.

Several months later, Eddie called asking if Johnnie would be interested in presenting him in concert, whose listening audience was way ahead of the nation in being Eddie Cochran fans, with his recordings being a regular feature on Rook's radio show. They agreed that he'd appear in both Hot Springs, South Dakota and Chadron, Nebraska.

Having just completed a survey of the record stores, Johnnie was pleased that Eddie had been voted at the top of the popularity polls of the record buying public. Rook had a trophy made, announcing Eddie as the area's number one singer, planning that the Keys to the City of Chadron and Hot Springs be given to him upon his arrival. The Nebraska appearance would be on Cochran's 21st birthday, so his fans would present him with a giant birthday cake. Little did they know that it would sadly be Eddie's last.

Both concerts were sell-outs, as fans from all over the area came to celebrate Cochran's birthday by attending the concert. Eddie wearing white bucks, with their tongue hanging out for comfort, put on great shows, being delighted not only to see Johnnie but by the welcome he'd helped arrange for him.

After both appearances they had some time alone, laughing over past experiences then talking about the future. Eddie encouraged Rook to "take your act to a larger town", having thought Denver and Salt Lake City would be excellent stepping stones for him to some day return to Los Angeles. They joked that an advancement in Johnnie's career would improve Cochran's too, Eddie saying, "We both need to move up some boy".

They toasted their friendship by swigging alcohol from a bottle that came out of nowhere. It would be their last time together, as Cochran told Rook about an upcoming tour of England planned for winter-spring of the following year. Johnnie thought how unusual it was for Eddie to be actually looking forward to traveling abroad to the UK, contrasting with how he'd felt before his tour of Australia.

Cochran's excitement over the trip was fueled by his being one of the first American rock acts to appear there. He told Rook about a new all black leather stage outfit he was planning to wear, that would come apart in pieces if grabbed by fans. Eddie joked that he was thinking about wearing nothing underneath the leather, saying "Can you imagine the attention that would get?"

Eddie walked Johnnie to his car, reminded him of their plans for seeing each other the following summer, when he would holiday in California. As they hugged goodbye, Johnnie kidded that he had every intention of being employed in radio in Los Angeles by then. Cochran's final words to Rook were, "You'll be staying out at the house with us, won't ya"? Eddie was proud of the new home he'd just bought for his parents in Buena Park, having been looking forward to Johnnie's visit, when he'd be his guest. Johnnie then waved goodbye to Eddie ….for the final time.

During mid March Alice phoned Rook, saying Eddie was having a very successful tour of England but "The bad part is Eddie's being held over for longer than he thought". Johnnie asked about Cochran's health, learning that his voice was scratchy from all the singing, later recalling thinking that he probably had his bottle of whiskey and honey handy.

Alice had hoped that he'd be home in time for Easter but didn't think it would happen, as he was being held over by the promoters, saying, "I guess they just love him over there Johnnie but he'll be ready for the desert, you can bet on that!" Rook told her to tell Eddie that he was proud of his successful tour of England and was looking forward to hearing from him once he returned to the States.

The ringing of the phone woke Johnnie on Easter Sunday morning. It was his brother Charles, who was working a weekend shift at KOBH, who began, "Did you know Cochran died?" Momentarily stunned, Johnnie told him to stop being smart, as he repeated, "No man! Eddie got killed in a car wreck in England".

Rook asked him to repeat, hearing the words again then hanging up the phone with tears streaming down his cheeks, beginning to leaf through his address book to find the new phone number for Eddie's home in Buena Park. Dialing in desperation, the line was busy but within a few minutes he could hear it ringing then Gloria answering with a weak "Hello".

"Is it true?" Johnnie asked without identifying himself. "Yes Johnnie, I'm afraid so" she replied, as her sobbing increased before Red came on the line. "Johnnie can you come out?" he asked. Rook answered, "I'm on my way Red" then hung up the phone. During a stopover in Denver, he telephoned Red again to let him know his arrival time in Los Angeles. As usual, he'd pick Johnnie up at the airport.

Red was waiting at the gate as Rook arrived, they shook hands as he grabbed Johnnie's suitcase then they walked silently to his car in the parking lot. Eddie's body hadn't yet arrived from England, so it would be two days with the family living in utter disbelief that Eddie was gone before any funeral.

Alice broke into tears upon Rook entering the house then putting her arms around his waist, stood for several minutes weeping in silence. She led Johnnie into Eddie's bedroom then they both sat down on the bed as Alice asked, "It just doesn't seem possible Johnnie, Eddie's gone". He comforted her before she stood, shaking her head saying, "I worried something like this would happen".

Rook rose from the bed then suddenly remembered his pledge to Eddie about looking after his mother, should anything happen to him. He thought how strange it was that Eddie had had a premonition of his own death. Johnnie leaned down to hug her again then they walked together into the silence of the living room, where they sat without saying anything for several minutes. The ringing phone broke the silence as Alice asked Rook to answer it. It was a call from the airline stating when they could expect Eddie's body to arrive in Los Angeles. Johnnie repeated the information out loud for Alice and Red, who'd entered the room, to hear.

Eddie's brother Bob arrived then began blaming the driver of the taxi in which Cochran was being transferred to the airport. Someone had told him that the car had a flat tyre, resulting in it careering out of control. Bob was furious as he said the car must have been traveling too fast or the driver must've been intoxicated. Gloria interrupted, "Well we just don't know what happened yet", asking Bob to stop talking about the tragedy in front of his mother.

Red and Bob met the flight Eddie's body was on at the airport then accompanied the casket to the funeral home, where they were first to view him. As they entered the house Bob said over and over, "It didn't look at all like Eddie". Either he was hoping it wasn't Eddie and all this was a bad dream, or was angry at the funeral home in England, so it was decided that a closed casket funeral should take place.

Gloria volunteered to miss the funeral, so that someone would be on hand at home to answer the constantly ringing telephone. Johnnie interrupted, insisting she attend the funeral with the family, saying he'd stay to answer the phone. Red asked if Rook would like to pay his last respects to Eddie with a private visit to the funeral home, which he did, so he drove Johnnie to the funeral home, where he then realized he'd like to remember Eddie as he knew him, not by viewing his remains.

Rook sat quietly for the better part of an hour beside Eddie's closed casket, remembering their days together in the past. Red entered the room, putting his hand on Johnnie's shoulder, asking if he was ready to leave. He stood then placed both of his hands on the casket, saying goodbye to his friend Eddie, before turning then walking from the room.

Eddie was laid to rest at Forest Lawn Cypress, where his brother Bob and his father Frank soon joined him. Frank Cochran, it seemed to Johnnie, had always been silently despondent, with Bob being obviously heartbroken, having begun to drink heavily.

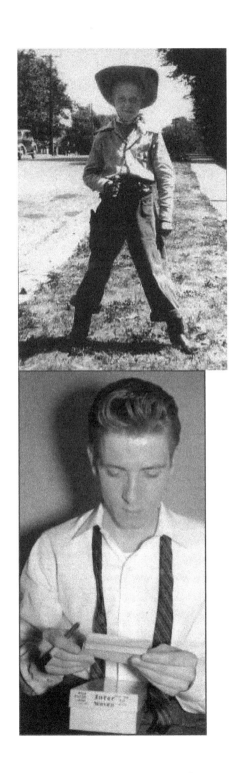

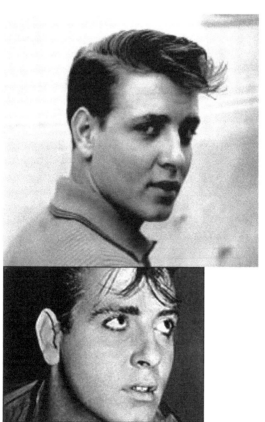

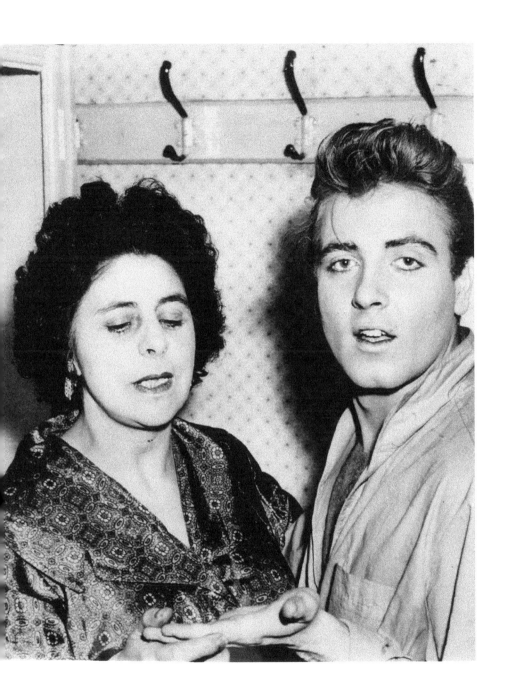

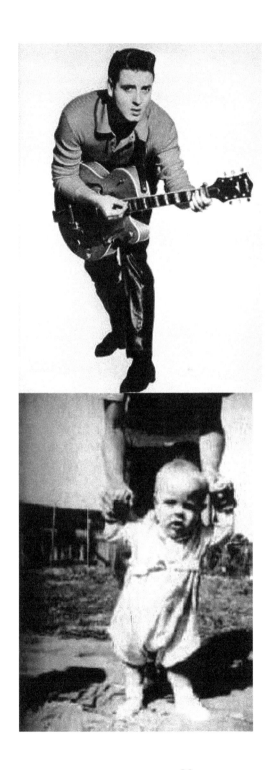

CPSIA information can be obtained
at www.ICGtesting.com
Printed in the USA
LVHW071710110919
630669LV00022BA/102/P